My Indian family history

Vic Parker

www.heinemann.co.uk/library
Visit our website to find out more information about Heinemann Library books.

To order:
☎ Phone 44 (0) 1865 888066
▤ Send a fax to 44 (0) 1865 314091
💻 Visit the Heinemann Bookshop at www.heinemann.co.uk/library to browse our catalogue and order online.

First published in Great Britain by Heinemann Library, Halley Court, Jordan Hill, Oxford OX2 8EJ, part of Harcourt Education. Heinemann is a registered trademark of Harcourt Education Ltd.

© Harcourt Education Ltd 2008
The moral right of the proprietor has been asserted.

Editorial: Charlotte Guillain
Design: Joanna Hinton-Malivoire
Picture research: Erica Martin
Production: Duncan Gilbert
Illustrated by Jacqueline McQuade
Originated by Modern Age
Printed and bound in China by South China Printing Co. Ltd.

ISBN 978 0 4310 1507 1 (hardback)
ISBN 978 0 4310 1502 6 (paperback)

12 11 10 09 08
10 9 8 7 6 5 4 3 2 1

British Library Cataloguing in Publication Data
Parker, Vic
My Indian family history. - (Family histories)
305.9'06912
A full catalogue record for this book is available from the British Library.

Acknowledgements
The publishers would like to thank the following for permission to reproduce photographs:
© Alamy pp. **17** (Simon Reddy), **24**, **26** (Ian Shaw); © Corbis pp. **11** (Bettmann), **21** (Reuters/Rupak De Chowdhuri); © Mary Evans Picture Library pp. **16**, **19**, **25**; © Getty Images pp. **12** (Time Life Picture/Jack Birns), **20** (Hulton Archive); © Robert Harding Picture Library p. **9** (John Henry Claude Wilson); © popperfoto.com p. **15**

Cover photograph of girl reproduced with permission of © Punchstock (Uppercut RF).

Every effort has been made to contact copyright holders of any material reproduced in this book. Any omissions will be rectified in subsequent printings if notice is given to the publishers.

Contents

Words appearing in the text in bold, **like this**, are explained in the Glossary.

My name is Savita. I am eight years old. I live with my mother, father, and older brother in a city called London.

London is England's **capital** city.

4

India is in South Asia, near Pakistan, China, Nepal, and Bangladesh.

My family comes from a country called India. India is one of the biggest countries in the world. It has hot deserts, steamy **rainforests**, and snowy mountains.

My family tree

My mother's parents

Bhupendra Patel
(my grandfather)
born 1926

Kamala Patel
(my grandmother)
born 1931

My father's parents

Govind Patel
(my grandfather)
born 1930

Deepika Patel
(my grandmother)
born 1933

Patel is a popular surname in Gujarat.

My grandparents grew up in India. One of my grandfathers, Bhupendra Patel, was born in a part of the country called Gujarat. Gujarat is by the sea. It is extremely dry and hot in summer.

My grandfather lived with his parents, three brothers, and two sisters in a small town.

My grandfather's town did not have electricity and people had to draw water from a well. My great-grandfather was a businessman. The family house was not very big. It had a kitchen, a living room, two bedrooms, and an outdoor toilet.

My great-grandmother could not read or write. But my great-grandfather thought school was very important. He made my grandfather work hard at lessons and do lots of extra study at home. My grandfather did not have much time to play.

At home my grandfather spoke a language called Gujarati. At school he also learned English.

This is the Hindu Temple of Somnath in Gujarat.

My grandfather and his family were **Hindus**, like many other people in India. They often went to a temple to pray. Every day, they prayed at a **shrine** in their home too.

My grandfather and his family went to one of India's busiest cities, Mumbai. They arrived with hardly any belongings or clothes. My grandfather and his brothers found work in a factory for very little money. The family had to live in a tin shack.

My grandfather and his family were very poor in Mumbai.

It was usual in those days for a **Hindu** bride and groom not to meet each other before their wedding.

My grandfather managed to finish his studies and become a doctor. When he was 32 years old, he married another doctor, called Kamala. Their families had arranged the marriage. My grandfather and Kamala met for the first time at their wedding.

My family tree

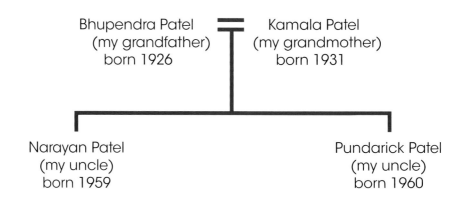

Bhupendra Patel
(my grandfather)
born 1926

Kamala Patel
(my grandmother)
born 1931

Narayan Patel
(my uncle)
born 1959

Pundarick Patel
(my uncle)
born 1960

My grandmother moved in with my grandfather and his family. The couple soon had a baby boy. A year later, another baby boy was born. The growing family was very crowded and it was hard to make ends meet.

My grandmother's brother was living in Britain. He had gone there in 1947 to escape the fighting between people in India and Pakistan. Now he invited my grandfather to go and live in Britain with him. In 1961, my grandfather set off for England on a boat.

People took all their belongings from India to Britain.

My grandmother's brother lived in London. My grandfather stayed with him until he got a job as a doctor in a hospital. Then he rented a room on his own. Finding a room took a long time, because a lot of English people didn't want to rent a room to an Indian person.

More and more people from India were coming to live in Britain.

This is a *thali*, which is a typical Gujarati meal.

My grandfather found Britain cold and strange. When he spoke, people could not understand his **accent**. Meals in the hospital canteen were often made with meat. Like a lot of **Hindus**, my grandfather was **vegetarian**, so he couldn't eat this sort of food.

My family tree

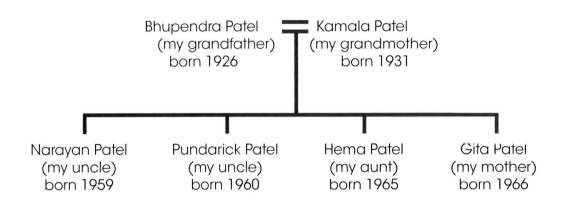

Bhupendra Patel
(my grandfather)
born 1926

Kamala Patel
(my grandmother)
born 1931

Narayan Patel
(my uncle)
born 1959

Pundarick Patel
(my uncle)
born 1960

Hema Patel
(my aunt)
born 1965

Gita Patel
(my mother)
born 1966

My grandfather saved money to bring my grandmother and their two sons to England. They rented a flat in a part of London called Harrow, where other Indian **Hindus** were living. They had two more children, both daughters.

At my mother's school, most of the children were white. Her best friend was a girl called Karen. Their favourite toys were Sindy dolls and space hoppers.

My mother was British, because she was born in Britain like her best friend, Karen.

Karen

My grandmother always wore a traditional Indian dress, called a sari. For special occasions, such as family celebrations and **Hindu** festivals, my mother wore a sari too. But she usually wore English clothes, like jeans and jumpers.

A sari is a long piece of cloth. You wrap one end around your waist to form a skirt. Then you drape the other end over your shoulders and head.

Diwali means "row of lights".

My mother's favourite Hindu festival was Diwali. People celebrate with coloured lights, candles, and fireworks. My mother enjoyed eating special sweets made from milk.

My mother and father had a big wedding party that lasted for three days.

My mother went to university and became a **chemist**. My grandparents introduced her to their friends' son. His name was Vijay and he was a **lawyer**. After a year getting to know each other, they got married.

My mother and father moved into their own house in Harrow. It was close to their parents' homes, so they could often all get together to share meals. Soon my mother and father had two children – my brother, Tushar, and then me!

My family tree

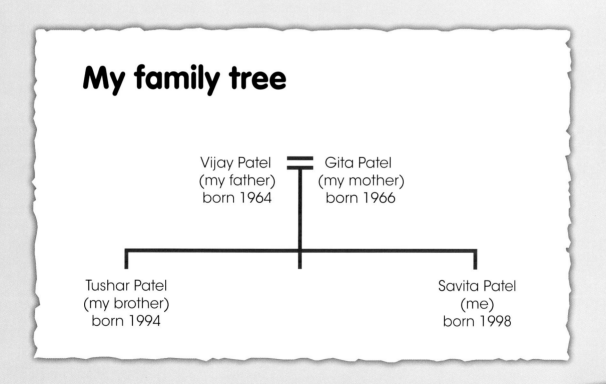

Vijay Patel
(my father)
born 1964

Gita Patel
(my mother)
born 1966

Tushar Patel
(my brother)
born 1994

Savita Patel
(me)
born 1998

I have grown up in Harrow. My friends at school have families from all over the world, including India. I would like to visit India one day.

I took this photograph of some of my school friends.

When I grow up I would like to dance and sing in an Indian film.

At school, my brother is studying an Indian instrument called the *tabla*. I am learning an Indian style of dancing called *kathak*. My school puts on a show every year and all my family comes to watch.

My grandfather sat on the floor at school and leaned a few subjects, including English. At my school we learn about many things, including *kathak* dancing.

When my grandfather came to Britain, it was unusual to see people from India. Now there are families from India and many other countries living all over Britain.

More books to read

Celebrations: Divali, Denise Jordan (Raintree, 2003)

Prita Goes to India, Prodeepta Das (Frances Lincoln, 2005)

Traditional Tales from India, Victoria Parker (Belitha Press, 2001)

We're from India, Victoria Parker (Heinemann Library, 2005)

Websites

www.bbc.co.uk/history/walk/memory_index.shtml
This website gives you tips on finding out about your own family history.

http://pbskids.org/wayback/family/tree/index.html
This website helps you to put together your own family tree.

Glossary

accent way people from a certain area pronounce words

capital a country's capital city is its most important city

chemist person whose job is to prepare medicines

Hindu person who follows the Hindu religion

lawyer person whose job is to make sure people follow a country's laws

rainforest type of jungle found in hot, rainy places

refugee person who has had to leave their home and everything behind, because they are in danger

shrine special place set aside for people to go to pray – sometimes with a holy picture or statue in it

vegetarian if you are vegetarian, you do not eat meat

Index